Hello Kitty®

Painting
Activity Book

Hello Kitty
& Her Friends
Crafts Club

by **Judy Lipsitt**

Scholastic Inc.

New York Toronto London Auckland Sydney
Mexico City New Delhi Hong Kong Buenos Aires

Designers: Peggy Gardner, Lee Kaplan
Illustrations: Yancey Labat

ISBN: 0-439-32846-2

12 11 10 9 8 7 6 5 4 3 2 1   2 3 4 5 6 7/0

Printed in the U.S.A.
First Scholastic printing, July 2002

Table of Contents

Painting Is Fun!

Hello Kitty loves to paint! She loves the excitement of creating new colors and shapes, and she loves experimenting with different ways to make a picture. Mostly, Hello Kitty loves to make paintings of all the fun things she does every day.

Join Hello Kitty and her pal Jody as they share with you painting activities of the fun they have all year long: picking apples in the fall, sledding in the winter, watering the garden in the spring, and paddling a canoe in the summer. Each season, Hello Kitty and Jody do so many exciting things that can be painted.

The projects in this book are sure to spark your imagination! Ready to paint? Let's go!

Get Ready to Paint with Hello Kitty

Along with this activity book, you also get a set of 18 watercolors, a paintbrush, and some very special Hello Kitty watercolor crayons. You'll learn how to use your special crayons on page 6.

Here are some tips to keep in mind before you start painting:

- Use a smock or an old shirt to keep your clothes clean.

- Spread out newspaper on the surface where you'll be painting so you don't make a mess.

- The best kind of paper to paint on is special watercolor paper, which you can get from an arts and craft store. Any other thick paper will work as well (although regular white paper won't, since it's thin and can tear).

- To clean your brush when you switch colors, borrow a bowl from your kitchen (be sure to ask for permission first) and fill it with water. Change the water when it gets muddy from the paint.

- Sometimes it's useful to mix paint colors to either create a new color or to change the hue of an existing color. To do this, you'll need a palette. Your palette can be the cover of your paint set, a small saucer, some cardboard, or a traditional painter's palette which can be found in an arts and crafts store.

  - To use your watercolor paints, dip your brush in water, then dab it around in one color until the paint is wet.

- In order to "paint a background" for a lot of the projects, you need a bigger paintbrush than the one that came with this kit so you'll be able to do this more easily.

  - To mix colors, make a patch of one color on your palette, then rinse your brush and dip it in a second color. Mix this with the first color. Keep mixing until you get the color you want. (Test your new color on scrap paper before painting with it.)

- After painting with one color, be sure to let the paint dry, or blot it with a tissue, before you put another color alongside or on top of it. Otherwise, the colors on your painting could run together.

- When you're finished painting, wash your brush in clean water, and wash and wipe your palette and paints. Don't forget to clean your work area!

Hello Kitty
Painting Projects

Before you get started painting pictures, Hello Kitty and Jody want to show you some super-special ways to use watercolor paints!

Super-duper Splatter Painting:

Splatter paint is a fun way to make a crazy design on your painting. Use lots of colors for a wild effect!

What You Do:

1. If you like, paint a background for your splatter-paint project. Then, let it dry.

What You Need:

- Paint
- Paintbrush
- Bowl of water
- Paper
- Palette

2. Dip your brush in the water, then make a large puddle of paint in any color you like on your palette (see page 3). Then dip your paintbrush in it, getting it very wet. Hold the brush over your paper and tap it several times so that the paint splatters. To make larger splatters, shake the brush up and down.

3. Make a puddle of another color of paint on your palette. Dip your brush in it, getting it very wet, and splatter it over your paper like you did in step 2.

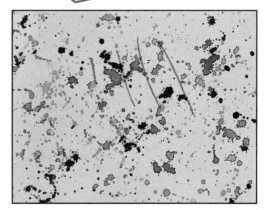

4. Continue splattering on colors until you finish with your design.

Hello Kitty **says**

Splatter painting is lots of fun, but it sure can be messy! Don't forget to lay down lots of newspaper.

Crazy Crayons:

It's time to test out your watercolor crayons! Experiment with your crayons, like Hello Kitty does, to find out what you like to do.

What You Do:

1. Start by drawing a design on your paper with your crayons. You can draw wiggly lines, dots, stars, hearts. Whatever strikes your fancy!

2. Now, wet your paintbrush in any color you like and begin painting over the shapes you just drew. If you paint lightly, the crayon shape won't mix, but if you press down a little harder, the crayon shape will start to blend like watercolor paint.

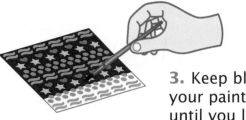

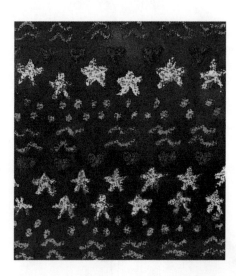

3. Keep blending your paintings until you like your design.

What You Need:

- Paper
- Crayons
- Paintbrush
- Bowl of water
- Paint

Funky Fingerprints:

It's time to get messy as Hello Kitty shows you one of her favorite painting techniques.

What You Do:

1. Wet your brush, then move it around in any color you want on your paint set until it's wet.

2. Put your finger on the selected wet paint pan. Move your finger around until it's coated with paint.

3. Then, use your paint-covered finger to make fingerprints on your paper.

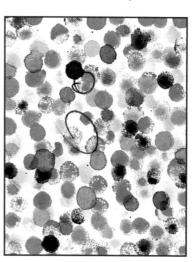

4. Rinse off your finger, then rinse your brush and wet another color of paint. Now make more fingerprints with this color.

5. Keep changing colors until your design is complete.

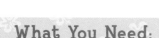

What You Need:

- Bowl of water
- Paintbrush
- Paint
- Paper

Hello Kitty says

You can use these techniques to liven up any painting.

Portraits of Hello Kitty and Jody:

Hello Kitty likes to find fun ways to paint portraits of herself and her friends. Would you like to try?

What You Do:

1. Trace Hello Kitty and Jody from page 40. (Sketch lightly so you only have a soft outline.)

2. Wet your black paint thoroughly with your paintbrush by mixing it with water and then dab your finger in it. Following your outline, press your finger around Hello Kitty and Jody's bodies. Add black dots on their eyes and outline their clothing. Rewet your paint as needed.

3. Rinse off your finger, then wet another color to fill in Hello Kitty's dress. How about making a pretty multicolored pattern? You'll need to rinse off your finger each time you switch colors.

4. Use your pink or red paint to dab on a pattern for Hello Kitty's bow.

What You Need:

- Tracing paper
- Pencil
- Paper
- Bowl of water
- Paintbrush
- Paint

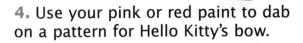

5. Use your brown paint to fill in Jody's body. Rewet the paint as needed.

6. You can make Jody's pants and shirt different colors, or make them multicolored. Whatever you like!

Hello Kitty **says**

Why not make finger-paint portraits of your friends and family?

Fall Fun

Fall is one of Hello Kitty's favorite seasons. Not only is her birthday in the fall, but there are also so many exciting things to do!

Hello Kitty Goes Apple Picking:

It's harvest time! Hello Kitty loves to go apple picking with her pal Jody.

What You Do:

1. Trace Hello Kitty and Jody from page 41 onto your paper. In pencil, draw an apple basket and fill it with some apples using your red crayon.

What You Need:

- Tracing paper
- Pencil
- Paper
- Crayons
- Paint
- Paintbrush
- Bowl of water
- Black marker

2. Draw an apple tree lightly with your pencil. Use your red crayon to make some apples on the tree.

3. Paint the leaves on your apple tree. While the paint is still wet, dab it with blobs of darker paint to add some texture to it.

4. Paint the tree trunk.

5. Paint the apple basket a cream color. When it's dry, outline it in brown paint or crayon.

6. Use your paints to color in Hello Kitty and Jody any way you like. When they're all dressed, outline them with black marker.

Hello Kitty **says**

With real yummy apples, you can make lots of cool treats, like applesauce and candy apples!

Hello Kitty and Her Kite:

On windy days, Hello Kitty loves flying her kite! Up, up, and away!

What You Do:

1. Trace Hello Kitty from page 41 onto your paper. Sketch her scarf and her kite.

2. Draw outlines of fluffy clouds in the sky with a pencil and color them in with your white crayon.

What You Need:

- Tracing paper
- Pencil
- Paper
- Crayons
- Paint
- Paintbrush
- Bowl of water
- Black marker

3. Color the sky. Be careful as you paint around Hello Kitty and her kite.

4. Pick a color for your kite and paint it in.

5. Paint the ground for Hello Kitty to stand on. How about using green?

6. Dress Hello Kitty with your paints. Decorate her clothing any way you like.

7. Once your painting is dry, outline Hello Kitty and her kite with a black marker.

Hello Kitty **says**

What other fun outdoor activities do you like to do in the fall? Bike? Jog? Hike? Why not paint scenes of these?

Happy Halloween, Hello Kitty:

**One of the most exciting times in the fall is Halloween—
and that means jack-o'-lanterns!**

What You Do:

1. Using a pencil, sketch a pumpkin on your paper like the one here.

2. Crazy eyes, a nose, and a mouth on the pumpkin turn it into a jack-o'-lantern. Color in the eyes with yellow and black crayons. Fill in the nose and mouth with just the yellow crayon. If you like, use your white crayon to add teeth, and color in some eyebrows with your yellow or black crayon.

3. Use a palette to mix orange and yellow paint to make a bright orange color, and paint your jack-o'-lantern with it. While it's still wet, add some yellow paint to highlight parts of it.

What You Need:

- Pencil
- Paper
- Crayons
- Palette
- Paint
- Paintbrush
- Bowl of water

4. When your jack-o'-lantern is dry, use your green crayon to define parts of it.

5. Use your dark green paint to color in the stem. When it's dry, outline the stem with your green crayon.

6. Now use some paint to make rosy cheeks for your jack-o'-lantern, if you like.

Hello Kitty **says**

You can paint lots of small jack-o'-lanterns on cards and give them to your friends to wish them a Happy Halloween.

Happy Birthday, Hello Kitty:

Hello Kitty's birthday is on November 1. Jody has planned an exciting birthday party for her. Would you like to come?

What You Do:

1. Using a pencil, sketch a party scene, like the one pictured, by starting with a table and chairs. Don't forget a birthday cake for Hello Kitty.

2. Trace Hello Kitty and Jody from page 41 into the scene you just drew. Give them some party hats.

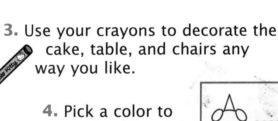

3. Use your crayons to decorate the cake, table, and chairs any way you like.

4. Pick a color to paint the cake and table.

What You Need:

- Pencil
- Paper
- Tracing paper
- Crayons
- Paint
- Paintbrush
- Bowl of water
- Palette
- Black marker

5. Now, paint some pretty candles onto the cake.

6. Mix some gold, brown, and orange paint in a palette and paint Jody.

7. Paint Jody's clothes any color you like. Don't forget to paint his party hat!

8. Now paint and decorate Hello Kitty, her dress, and her party hat any way you like.

9. Outline Hello Kitty and Jody with black marker once the paint has dried.

Hello Kitty **says**

Birthdays are great fun! When is your birthday?

Winter Wonderland

It can get very cold in winter, but it sure is great when it snows!

Let It Snow!:

Hello Kitty and Jody have so much fun in the snow. Today, they want to go sledding!

What You Do:

1. Sketch the background of your winter scene. How about some pretty mountains? Then, use your white crayon to draw some snow falling. Paint the sky.

2. Mix some gray, white, and blue paint in a palette to make a pale snow color. Paint this over the mountain and background.

What You Need:

- Pencil
- Paper
- Crayons
- Paint
- Paintbrush
- Bowl of water
- Palette
- Tracing paper
- Black marker

18

3. Now you're ready to draw Hello Kitty and Jody. Trace them from the patterns on page 42. Sketch a sled for Jody to sit on. Use your crayons and paints to make everything come alive.

4. Once your painting has dried, outline Hello Kitty and Jody with a black marker.

Hello Kitty says

What else can you do in the snow? Build a snow person, make snow angels, and slide on the ice!

Winter Diorama:

What better way to show an exciting ski scene than by using a diorama! These 3-D displays help Hello Kitty and Jody show off their super ski techniques!

What You Do:

1. Cut a piece of paper 11" by 7". Then cut a second piece of paper 10" by 5", and a third 9" by 4". Ask a grown-up to help you.

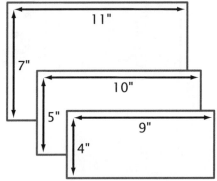

2. Think of a scene for your diorama. What about Hello Kitty on skis and Jody building a snowman? Now paint the background part of the scene on the biggest piece of paper. This should be things that are the farthest away in the scene—like mountains and clouds.

What You Need:

- Scissors
- Paper
- Ruler
- Paint
- Paintbrush
- Bowl of water
- Tracing paper
- Black marker
- Stapler

3. On the second largest piece of paper, paint the middle ground part of your scene. These are things that aren't quite as far away as things in the background, but aren't really close to you, such as trees and smaller ski slopes.

4. On the smallest piece of paper, paint the foreground of your scene. This means things that are closest to the front of your picture. Trace Hello Kitty and Jody from page 42 onto your paper, standing on snowy ground, and paint them in. How about adding a snowman? When they're dry, outline them with a black marker.

5. When the paint is dry, use your scissors to carefully cut off the top of the middle ground scene, then the top of the foreground scene.

6. Put all three parts together from small to large. Line them all up evenly on the right side and staple them together.

7. Bend the pieces of paper slightly so you're able to line up all three pieces on the left side, and staple them together. Now your diorama is ready to stand!

Hello Kitty's Pop-up Valentine:

Hello Kitty celebrates Valentine's Day by making cards for all her friends. You can, too!

What You Do:

1. Start by tracing the heart pattern on page 43 onto your paper.

2. Paint your valentine any way you like. Why not paint a pink heart in the middle of the valentine and a bigger red heart around it?

3. Now color in Hello Kitty with your paints. Let the paint dry.

4. With a black marker, outline Hello Kitty and the center heart shape, if you drew one, and write a special message on your valentine with your markers.

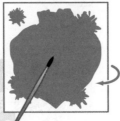

5. Turn your valentine over and paint the back of it. You only need to paint enough to go around the heart shape. Now, let this side dry.

What You Need:

- Pencil
- Tracing paper
- Paper
- Paint
- Paintbrush
- Bowl of water
- Markers
- Scissors

6. Use your scissors to carefully cut out the valentine pattern.

22

7. Fold the valentine in half so that Hello Kitty's face is inside the fold. Then, open the valentine and fold it in half the other way so that her face is on the outside of the fold.

8. With the card still folded in half, follow the diagonal dotted lines from the pattern to carefully fold one side of Hello Kitty's head forward. Run over the fold with your nail to make it very clean.

9. Then fold Hello Kitty's head in the *opposite* direction, again using your nail to sharpen the fold.

10. Now fold the entire card inward. Make sure that Hello Kitty folds down *into* the card, as shown here. When you open the card, Hello Kitty pops up! Your card is ready to share!

Happy Valentine's Day!

Hello Kitty **says**

Make lots of valentines and send them to your favorite friends!

Dancing on Ice:

When Hello Kitty ice-skates, she dances across the ice, spinning and gliding!

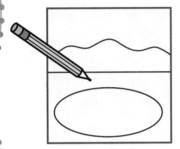

What You Do:

1. Start by sketching the background of your picture. Sketch a pretty mountain and a pond for Hello Kitty to skate on.

2. Trace Hello Kitty from page 42 onto your paper. Draw her a warm hat and scarf, and sketch some ice skates. Why not add a flower on her hat?

What You Need:
- Pencil
- Paper
- Tracing paper
- Paint
- Paintbrush
- Bowl of water
- Palette
- Black marker
- White poster paint

3. Use your blue or purple paint to fill in the sky above the mountain. Then use your gray paint to color in the mountain.

4. Mix some gray paint with water on your palette. Make it a lighter shade than the gray you used on the mountain. Now color in the ground and the pond with it.

5. Color in Hello Kitty and her outfit any way you like.

6. When the paint is dry, use a black marker to outline Hello Kitty.

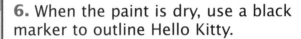

7. Let it snow! Use the splatter paint technique (see pages 4–5) and some white poster paint to make snow all over your picture for the finishing touch.

Hello Kitty **says**

Skating is fun! You can ice-skate in winter and in-line skate the rest of the year.

Spring Fever

Spring is the season when everything comes to life again!

April Showers:

It's raining! It's pouring! Good thing Hello Kitty brought her umbrella!

What You Do:

1. Start by sketching the background of your picture. Where will Hello Kitty be this time? Sketch some rainclouds for your setting.

2. Trace Hello Kitty holding her umbrella, from page 43, onto your paper.

What You Need:

- **Pencil**
- **Paper**
- **Tracing paper**
- **Crayons**
- **Paint**
- **Paintbrush**
- **Bowl of water**
- **Palette**
- **Black marker**

3. Now you're ready to start coloring in your picture. Fill in the rainclouds with your white crayon.

4. Mix some gray paint with water on your palette to make a light gray, then color in the sky. When it's dry, use regular gray or black paint to draw drops of rain.

5. Use your paints to color in Hello Kitty, her clothes, and her umbrella any way you like. Once she's dry, outline Hello Kitty and her umbrella with a black marker.

Hello Kitty says

April showers bring May flowers!

Rainbow Kitty:

After the rain, a beautiful rainbow follows. Hello Kitty and Jody love chasing after rainbows!

What You Do:

1. Trace the picture of Hello Kitty and Jody from page 41 onto your paper.

2. Paint Hello Kitty and Jody any way you like.

3. Once Hello Kitty and Jody are dry, outline them with a black marker.

What You Need:

- Tracing paper
- Pencil
- Paper
- Paint
- Paintbrush
- Bowl of water
- Black marker
- Ruler

4. With a pencil, draw seven arched lines about ¼" apart (for the six colors of a rainbow).

5. Using your paints, paint the rainbow in the color order you see here.

Red, Orange, Yellow, Light Green, Blue, Purple

Hello Kitty **says**

What a colorful way to spend a spring day!

How Does Your Garden Grow?:

Hello Kitty loves her garden! She has lots of beautiful flowers.

What You Do:

1. Trace Hello Kitty from page 41 onto your paper. Sketch a pretty flower on her head. Then draw a flowerpot and some flowers for her like the ones here.

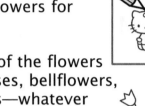

2. Draw the rest of the flowers in the garden: roses, bellflowers, daisies, and irises—whatever you like! Then paint them.

Roses

Bellflowers

Daisies

Irises

What You Need:

- Tracing paper
- Pencil
- Paper
- Paint
- Paintbrush
- Bowl of water
- Black marker

3. Paint all the leaves and stems using your green paint.

4. Now paint Hello Kitty. Don't forget to color her watering can and flowerpot!

5. Once your picture is dry, outline Hello Kitty and her watering can with a black marker to make them stand out.

Hello Kitty **says**

You can draw lots of other fun things in your garden, too, like birds, butterflies, and insects.

What's in the Pond, Hello Kitty?:

In Hello Kitty's garden, there is a little pond with water lilies, a fat green frog, and beautiful blue dragonflies.

What You Do:

1. Sketch water lilies, a frog, and some dragonflies (see page 42 for patterns) on your paper like the ones shown here.

2. Use your light blue paint to paint a pale blue sky in your picture.

3. When the sky is dry, paint each dragonfly's wings and body. Add paint for the eyes.

What You Need:

- Pencil
- Tracing paper
- Paper
- Paint
- Paintbrush
- Bowl of water
- Black marker

4. Now paint the lilies any bright color you like. Paint the lily pads a dark green.

5. Use your light green paint to color in the frog. Put dark green spots on its body. Don't forget to add the eyes!

6. Use your light and dark blue paint to color in the water.

7. When your painting is dry, outline the frog using a black marker.

Hello Kitty **says**

All summer long, you can splish-splash and paddle in all kinds of water!

Summertime Fun

Grab your sunglasses and some cool lemonade, Hello Kitty.
Summer is here!

Paddling Along:

Hello Kitty and Jody keep cool on a sunny day by paddling along in a canoe on a clear blue lake.

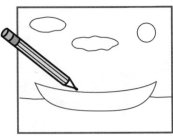

What You Do:

1. Lightly sketch clouds, sun, the lake, and a canoe on your paper.

2. Trace Hello Kitty and Jody from page 43 onto your paper so they fit into the canoe. Trace their paddles as well.

What You Need:

- Pencil
- Paper
- Tracing paper
- Crayons
- Paint
- Paintbrush
- Bowl of water
- Black marker

3. Use a white crayon to fill in the clouds. Paint the sky with your light blue paint. When the sky is dry, draw a bright yellow sun with your crayon. Then, use a wet brush to blend the color of the sun around it. This will make your sun glow.

4. Paint Hello Kitty and Jody. When Hello Kitty and Jody are dry, outline them with a black marker.

5. Paint the canoe and paddles any colors you like.

6. Use your dark blue, light blue, and purple paint to make the water.

Hello Kitty says

There's nothing like a fun day outdoors with a good friend!

Technicolor Fish:

Hello Kitty and Jody love brightly colored fish! You can find them at the aquarium, at sea, or in a great book!

What You Do:

1. Paint a piece of paper using any paint color you like, but keep in mind that this will be the sea for your picture.

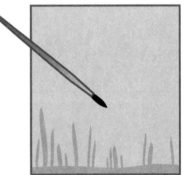

2. On another sheet of paper, sketch your fish. Color each fish shape with your paint.

What You Need:

- Paper
- Paint
- Paintbrush
- Bowl of water
- Pencil
- Bubble wrap (optional)
- Scissors
- Glue

3. Now it's time to decorate your fish! You can use any technique you like. You can use some bubble wrap and press a cool circle pattern to make scales for your fish. Or, you can use a finger-paint technique to add spots (see page 7). Splatter paint is another great way to add some color to your fish (see pages 4–5). Or, you can come up with your own fun technique.

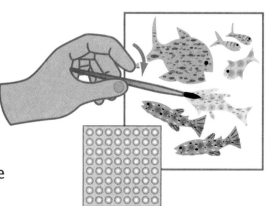

4. When you're done designing your fish, let them dry, and then cut them out.

5. Glue each fish onto the sea scene that you made in step 1, and hang up your picture wherever you like!

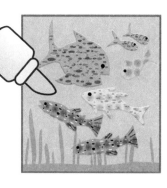

Hello Kitty **says**

There are all kinds of cool fish that live in the sea. Use your imagination to make up as many fun fish as you like!

Hello Kitty Wishes on a Star:

Before Hello Kitty goes to bed at night, she loves to look out her window at the shining moon and the twinkling stars. Then she closes her eyes and makes a wish. Do you do this, too?

What You Do:

1. Sketch Hello Kitty's window, with the stars and moon in the window. Add a plant on the windowsill for an extra-cute touch. Draw some curtains.

2. Trace Hello Kitty from page 43 onto your paper. Draw her a long nightgown and a special teddy bear.

3. Use a white crayon to color the stars. Paint the sky a dark blue. Paint the moon a bright yellow. When the moon is dry, go around it with a wet brush. Then paint a yellow circle on the wet section (the paint will blur like moonlight).

What You Need:

- Pencil
- Paper
- Tracing paper
- Crayons
- Paint
- Paintbrush
- Bowl of water
- Black marker

4. Paint the curtains a light blue, if you like. While they're wet, paint in folds with your darker blue paint.

5. Paint the wall whatever color or pattern you like.

6. Paint Hello Kitty's nightgown and bow. Paint her teddy bear and the flowerpot. Paint green leaves for the plant.

7. When your painting is dry, outline Hello Kitty and her teddy bear with black marker.

Hello Kitty says

I love going to bed in my cozy room and listening to the sounds of a summer night.

Hello Kitty
Shapes to Trace

For "Portraits of Hello Kitty and Jody" (pages 8–9)

**For "Hello Kitty Goes Apple
Picking" (pages 10–11)
and "Rainbow Kitty" (pages 28–29)**

**For "Hello Kitty and
Her Kite" (pages 12–13)**

**For "Happy Birthday, Hello Kitty"
(pages 16–17)**

**For "How Does Your
Garden Grow?"
(pages 30–31)**

For "Let It Snow!" (pages 18–19)

For "What's in the Pond, Hello Kitty?" (pages 32–33)

For "Dancing on Ice" (pages 24–25)

For "Winter Diorama" (pages 20–21)

For "Paddling Along" (pages 34–35)

For "Paddling Along" (pages 34–35)

For "April Showers" (pages 26–27)

For "Hello Kitty Wishes on a Star" (pages 38–39)

For "Hello Kitty's Pop-up Valentine" (pages 22–23)

Good-bye from Hello Kitty and Jody!

Painting can be so much fun! Now that you've made pictures with Hello Kitty and Jody, what other ideas can you come up with? How about a painting of you and Hello Kitty together on a sailboat or traveling to a foreign country? Use your imagination. The possibilities are endless!

Smooches,

xoxox

Hello Kitty and Jody